D1061144

THE WAR *of* 1812

A HISTORY PERSPECTIVES BOOK

Amy Van Zee

Published in the United States of America by Cherry Lake Publishing
Ann Arbor, Michigan
www.cherrylakepublishing.com

Consultants: Peter C. Vermilyea, Lecturer, History Department, Western Connecticut State University; Marla Conn, ReadAbility, Inc.
Editorial direction: Red Line Editorial
Book design and illustration: Sleeping Bear Press

Photo Credits: Library of Congress, cover (left), 1 (left), 19; F. C. Yohn/ Library of Congress, cover (middle), 1 (middle), 27; AP Images, cover (right), 1 (right), 25; North Wind/North Wind Picture Archives, 4, 5, 6, 11, 14, 15, 22, 30; N. Currier/Library of Congress, 26

Library of Congress Cataloging-in-Publication Data
Van Zee, Amy.
The War of 1812 / Amy Van Zee.
pages cm. – (Perspectives library)
ISBN 978-1-62431-424-7 (hardcover) – ISBN 978-1-62431-500-8 (pbk.) – ISBN 978-1-62431-462-9 (pdf) – ISBN 978-1-62431-538-1 (ebook)
1. United States–History–War of 1812–Juvenile literature. I. Title.
E354.V36 2013
973.5'2–dc23

2013006433

Cherry Lake Publishing would like to acknowledge the work of The Partnership for 21st Century Skills. Please visit *www.p21.org* for more information.

Printed in the United States of America
Corporate Graphics Inc.
July 2013
CLFA11

TABLE OF CONTENTS

In this book, you will read about the War of 1812 from three perspectives. Each perspective is based on real things that happened to real people who fought in or lived during the war. As you'll see, the same event can look different depending on one's point of view.

1

Thomas Williams

American Soldier

Again, we have taken up arms against the British! When our Congress declared war on June 18, 1812, I was ready to join the fight. For years, the British navy had been chasing down American ships and **impressing** seamen into their service. But the British went too far in the summer of 1807. That June, sailors on the British *Leopard* fired on our *Chesapeake* and boarded her. They believed the ship carried **deserters** from the British navy. The *Leopard* took four men and left the *Chesapeake* damaged. We were furious when we heard the news. The British were acting as if we were still their colonies! We could not sit by and let them abuse us so.

I followed the news closely to see how our government and President Thomas Jefferson would react. But the answers were not simple. Our nation

▲ *Impressment of Americans by the British was one cause of the War of 1812.*

was navigating the **trade restrictions** of France and Britain, who were fighting against each other. In 1806, France tried to destroy British trade through

American trade was hurt by British and French blockades. ▶

blockades. Britain then attempted to block French ports. Britain wanted any ship trading with France to come to Britain first and pay a fee. France responded by declaring that ships following British rules would be attacked as though they were British. How could our ships trade with Europe with such complicated restrictions? We were stuck between these two warring nations with no easy solution.

After the *Chesapeake* incident, our Congress responded with Jefferson's Embargo Act. American ships could no longer export goods under the terms of the act. I believe Jefferson hoped to show Britain and France that they needed our trade. Taking away trade with America would punish the French and British for their blockades and restrictions. But these new enactments hurt us more than anyone, for our nation became utterly cut off. East coast tradesmen suffered greatly from the decline in business. Many joined the cry for "Free Trade and Sailors' Rights."

In the following years, more trade restrictions came. Our relationship with the British grew worse.

For us here in the western parts of our new nation, we had different complaints against the British. They seemed to be supporting the Indians we encountered on the frontier. We heard about the powerful Shawnee chief Tecumseh and his brother Tenskwatawa. Rumors flew that Tecumseh was using his influence to unite the tribes against us to prevent America from expanding to the west.

In early November 1811, our forces were attacked by a **confederation** of Indians at the Tippecanoe River. We heard that the British had somehow encouraged the attack. We did not know their exact relationship with the Indians, but our anger against the British burned at this news. And after this

THINK ABOUT IT

▶ What is the main idea of this paragraph and the paragraph before it? What evidence in the paragraphs supports this main idea?

Battle of Tippecanoe, Tecumseh joined with the British outright. So we faced the British and the Indians together. In Congress, Henry Clay and other **War Hawks** shared our point of view as they pushed for war.

Many seemed ready to remove British influence from Canada as well as the seas, and there was talk that we could even take that nation from the British. Emotions ran high as we considered war with the nation we had won independence from just a few decades earlier.

For me and many others, this war was about our nation's honor. We wanted to show the British that we are an independent nation. As such, I joined the army. We gathered with other volunteers in Indiana in late summer of 1812. We heard whispers that we would push northward in an invasion of Canada. "On to Canada!" became our enthusiastic cry.

Although our spirits were high, things quickly took a turn for the worse. That autumn and the following winter brought terrible conditions. Snow and rain dampened our moods and chilled us to the bone. Many of my fellow soldiers did not have enough clothing to protect them from the howling wind, rain, and snow. Some even went barefoot. And food! We ate some pork and beef, but oh, how we

UNPREPARED FOR WAR

When the United States declared war in the summer of 1812, it had an army of 6,700 men and a navy of fewer than 20 ships. Volunteers were poorly trained and lacked experience. Not every state agreed about going to war either. Some New England states withheld money. The governors of Massachusetts and Connecticut even refused to let their men fight outside their own states.

▲ *American soldiers fought Tecumseh and tribes that had sided with the British.*

lacked enough. All around me, hundreds of men grew sick with typhus. Many died. I began to feel very frustrated that our government could not send supplies to help us. Some around me even spoke of desertion. Would we last the winter?

All the while, we had many encounters with the enemy. We often sent out spies to gather information about the Indians around us. On one occasion, our spies did not return for a few days. We feared the worst. We later learned they had come upon a group of Indians. The Indians **prevailed** and our men were scalped. On other occasions, our men brought back word that large groups of Indians were encamped near us. This brought more discouragement. On half **rations**, and with so few men, how would we defeat the enemy? To counter our fears, our officers rallied us with speeches. I remembered again my eagerness to fight for my country. Our high

SECOND SOURCE

▶ Find another source on this event and compare the information there to the information in this source. What else can you learn about the British and Indian perspectives of the battle at the River Raisin?

spirits returned and we were ready to press on. Our officers led us northward as we marched to the River Raisin in Monroe, Michigan.

What happened there in late January 1813 will haunt my memories for the rest of my life. We faced a strong line of British and Indian forces that began the attack with shots so loud I believed my ears would bleed. In the face of such strength, many of our soldiers panicked and fled. We saw the enemies advance on these poor men to finish them off. Determined to stand our ground, a group of us bravely rallied. Our rifles were our last resort. But our ammunition would not last against the mighty forces of our enemies. With anger, shock, and great despair, we had no choice but to surrender. Oh, how my heart ached for my nation. Will we crumble against the British forces at our doorstep? I pray our armies elsewhere and navy men have greater success than us.

2

Oliver Miller

British Soldier

Another war to fight, after so many years of fighting already behind us! When the United States declared war against us in 1812, the news caused great aggravation to my fellow soldiers and me. Our nation had been warring with Napoleon Bonaparte and his French forces almost constantly since 1793. That tyrant wants to rule the world, and his arrogance has already cost many lives. The war with Bonaparte has ravaged our nation, our families, and our military—especially our navy.

We need sailors. Rumors have spread that conditions are harsh on British ships. Many sailors have been impressed into service against their will. We even heard that some began to claim American citizenship to leave the British navy and sail on American ships, where they receive higher pay. But we must have strong forces on the seas if we are to face Bonaparte's navy! What choice do we have but to seek out these deserters, even if it

British sailors boarded American ships to find deserters. ▶

means boarding American ships to find them and bring them back?

Indeed, when our *Leopard* fired on the *Chesapeake* in 1807, at least one deserter was found among the four men who were taken. Are these actions not justified if we are to stop Bonaparte from taking over Europe? The Americans must not be so naïve as to think he would spare coming after them.

Yet the Americans seem to be singling us out as the enemy, at least as far as trade is concerned. Bonaparte intended to ruin us by blocking our trade with the rest of Europe. We responded by putting up blockades of French ports. French and British interference in trade angered American sailors, who risked seizure by France or us. But we had to prevent other countries from trading with France.

SECOND SOURCE

▶ Find another source that describes British action needed against Bonaparte and his French forces. How does the information there compare to what you read here?

In 1807, the United States passed the Embargo Act, which ended all its exports. Perhaps the Americans hoped to force us to end the blockades. We know our actions have hurt American trade, but Bonaparte's have as well. Yet they chose to declare war with us. Even in the face of Bonaparte's tyranny, the Americans are siding with their old ally.

So war it is. I myself did not join in the war with the Americans until 1814, for until then I was fighting on French soil. But our war with France ended that year, so my fellow soldiers and I sailed to America to aid the British troops already there. We arrived at the entrance to the Chesapeake Bay in early August. Our goal was to take Washington, the nation's capital city. On August 16, our fleet entered the bay and we began making our way up the Patuxent River toward our goal. On August 20, we landed on American soil.

It was my first time seeing America. A mixture of emotions welled up in my heart. I wanted to see these people humbled for their boldness in bringing another war upon us. Yet, not long ago they were British colonies. I still felt many ties to the people of this young nation.

As we left the ship, the heat was almost unbearable. My heavy wool uniform served me well through a French winter. Yet as we left the ship sweat poured off my forehead and soaked my back. Duty pressed me forward as we began the march toward Washington.

Although the physical toll of the march was great, we were surprised that we did not face resistance. We hardly saw a person during the five days it took us to arrive at Bladensburg, where we finally engaged the enemy on August 24. We were tired from our march, but the battle there was quick and decisive in our favor. Although the Americans put up a decent fight at first, after three short hours we saw them fleeing in retreat. My comrades and I, who had endured years of war against Bonaparte's forces, were experienced soldiers. We could not help but note how undisciplined these American troops seemed to be.

This battle was over, but we did not rest long. We had seven miles to march before we'd reach Washington, and the road before us was clear. When we arrived, the city was eerily quiet. Our men sent word to anyone remaining that peaceful citizens

▲ *British soldiers burned several buildings in Washington.*

would be respected, but it seemed nobody was there to hear the message. We had received our orders to burn public buildings. Although we had taken our enemy's capital city as our prize, I found no joy in obeying these orders.

I told myself that this was due payback. In 1813, the Americans took the Canadian city of York and

THE BIRTH OF A NATIONAL ANTHEM

After the Battle of Bladensburg and the burning of Washington, the British set their sights on Baltimore, an important U.S. port city. In September 1814, the British attacked Baltimore's Fort McHenry with rockets and cannons. American lawyer Francis Scott Key witnessed the fort's successful defense and was inspired to write a poem. His words became the lyrics to "The Star-Spangled Banner."

burned some of its buildings. The thought did not bring me peace though. It seemed my fellow soldiers felt the same as we set fire to the Capitol building and the president's home. Inside the house, flames consumed the furnishings, curtains, and carpets. It saddened me to see the destruction of property.

That night, the burning city lit up the black sky. I surveyed the destruction around me. My heart was heavy in my chest. I had seen enough war to last two lifetimes. I said a silent prayer that the burning of America's capital would bring about the end of the war. I had hoped we would quickly return to peaceful relations without more bloodshed. But that was not to be.

ANALYZE THIS

- Compare this British soldier's perspective with the perspective of the American soldier fighting in the Northwest. How are the two perspectives different? How are they similar?

James Scott

American Privateer

It is a relief to have another war with Britain behind us. As a New Englander living in Baltimore, I had mixed feelings about the conflict. In Baltimore, where the shipping industry reigns, many strongly supported the war. They knew how the British have treated our ships on the high seas. But most of the New England states opposed the war. Shipping is a great livelihood there as well. The men and women of those states feared the war would further damage the shipping industry. It had already suffered greatly from trade restrictions. Some of the states even threatened **secession**!

I had traveled to Baltimore to take my chances as a **privateer**. The government had issued **letters of marque and reprisal** to allow private shipowners to take part in the war. The letters essentially allowed us to become legal pirates. Our job was to capture British ships. I hoped that our efforts would harm British commerce and help our side win the war, and my heart leapt at the chance for adventure and the possibility of riches. We privateers would split the money made from any valuable cargo and goods our ship took.

I joined the crew of a fine ship, and we sailed from Baltimore. At sea, we practiced the skills to board an enemy ship and soon put our skills into action. When a sail was spotted, we chased it down as fast as we could. Often, the ship would show American colors, so we would leave it be. Some of the British ships we took did not put up a fight. But we engaged the enemy many times, firing a **broadside** with our large guns until the ship took down its colors and surrendered. Oh, the prizes we took! In the cargo holds of these ships we found rum, linen, furniture, tobacco, and other supplies. More than once we estimated a captured ship and its cargo to be worth more than $35,000. When we were not chasing down a prize, most of our time was spent in ship tasks and upkeep. But some evenings found us playing music, singing, and dancing. The general mood was good.

I admit that most of us were motivated by financial gain, not patriotism. But after we returned to port in late 1814, I sought out news of how our country was faring

ANALYZE THIS

▶ This privateer and the American soldier both acted on behalf of the United States. How did their motivations for being a part of the war differ?

▲ *Privateers chased British ships in order to take their supplies and valuables.*

against the British. It seemed both sides had won victories and faced losses. I learned our American army had suffered great defeats in the northwest as they attempted to invade Canada. Among the defeats, our forces had surrendered to British General Isaac Brock at Detroit in August 1812. And the British seemed to rule the Great Lakes until our Commodore Oliver Hazard Perry bravely led our navy to victory at the Battle of Lake Erie in September 1813.

Words cannot describe the sadness I felt when I learned the British had set fire to Washington in August 1814. But I took heart when I learned that our dear First Lady, Dolley Madison, escaped the city with some of our nation's important documents.

American forces defeated the British in the Battle of Lake Erie. ▼

On top of that, our forces had defended Baltimore the following month.

The final months of the war seemed to me to be pure confusion. After Washington and Baltimore, the British attempted to take New Orleans in January 1815. The famous British General Sir Edward Pakenham led the well-prepared British Army of almost 14,000 soldiers. In contrast, our side was made up of a rag-tag group of men commanded by Major General Andrew Jackson. About 4,000 roughly dressed soldiers, frontiersmen, free blacks, and pirates dug in to

Andrew Jackson led the Americans to victory over the British at the Battle of New Orleans in 1815. ▶

defend the city. It seemed the odds were against us. On January 8, the British troops advanced against our men. But Jackson had positioned his men well. The short battle resulted in a bitter defeat for the British. After so many disappointments, this victory was a great boost to our morale!

In mid-February, the news broke that a peace treaty had been signed in Europe. With this information, some believed that the recent victory at

THE TREATY OF GHENT

The peace treaty that ended the War of 1812 was signed in the city of Ghent, which is in present-day Belgium. The treaty did not officially stop impressment of American soldiers, which was one of the reasons behind the war. Historians still question which side won the War of 1812.

New Orleans had brought about the peace treaty. But that was not so. The treaty had been signed in late December 1814, before the battle there began.

So our minds raced with questions. Could the Battle of New Orleans have been prevented? Who really won the war? And though the treaty supposedly brought peace, it did not address the issues that caused the war in the first place. Will our ships be able to sail freely? Will our men be impressed into British service? It seems the treaty signers settled for a return to the way things were before the war, with no new agreements made. For my part, I truly hope that this treaty will be the means of bringing many peaceful years with the Canadians, the Indians, and the British across the sea.

SECOND SOURCE

▶ Find a source that describes a British, Canadian, or Indian perspective on the end of the war. Compare the perspective you find there with this one.

LOOK, LOOK AGAIN

This image shows the burning of Washington by the British. Use this image to answer the following questions:

1. How would an American soldier who was fighting in the Northwest react to hearing the news that British soldiers had burned Washington? How would he have thought the Americans should respond?

2. How would a British soldier describe this scene in a letter to his family back home?

3. If an American privateer saw this scene, what would he think about the British? Would his motivations for being a part of the war change? How so?

GLOSSARY

blockade (blah-KADE) the closing off of an area, such as a port, to keep supplies or people out

broadside (BRAWD-side) the firing of all the guns on one side of a ship

confederation (kuhn-fed-uh-RAY-shun) a union of people or groups acting together

deserter (di-ZUR-tur) a soldier who leaves his or her military duties without intending to come back

impress (im-PRES) to force a person into a country's navy

letters of marque and reprisal (LET-urs UHV MAHRK AND ri-PRYE-zuhl) documents allowing for people such as privateers to seize the property of enemies, especially during wartime

prevail (pri-VAYL) to overcome; to win

privateer (prye-vuh-TEER) a sailor on a private, armed ship that is allowed to attack other ships

ration (RASH-uhn) a specific amount of food and drink given to a soldier

secession (suh-SEH-shun) the act of leaving the Union

trade restriction (TRADE ri-STRIK-shun) the limiting or stopping of trade imposed by a government against another country

War Hawks (WOR HAWKS) the nickname given to men in Congress who pushed for war with the United Kingdom

LEARN MORE

Further Reading

Damanda, Lori. *The Story of the Star-Spangled Banner.* New York: PowerKids, 2009.
Isaacs, Sally Senzell. *What Caused the War of 1812?* New York: Crabtree, 2011.
Johnson, Robin. *Famous People of the War of 1812.* New York: Crabtree, 2011.

Web Sites

A Sailor's Life for Me
http://www.asailorslifeforme.org
From the USS Constitution Museum, this Web site contains an interactive game and information about life aboard the *Constitution* during the War of 1812.

The Star-Spangled Banner
http://amhistory.si.edu/starspangledbanner/default.aspx
This Web site hosts information about the "Star-Spangled Banner," including the background of the War of 1812 and the full poem that led to the song.

INDEX

ABOUT THE AUTHOR

Amy Van Zee is an editor and writer who lives with her family near Minneapolis, Minnesota. She has a bachelor's degree in English from the University of Minnesota and has contributed to dozens of educational books.